HYDROPONICS

Grow Herbs, Vegetables and Fruits at Home Without Soil

Sustainable Living LIfestyle

1

Introduction

Hydroponics is a method of growing plants without soil by delivering nutrients straight to the roots through a nutrient-rich water solution. The earliest documented usage of hydroponics can be traced back to the Hanging Gardens of Babylon, which are thought to have been built in the sixth century BCE.

"Hydroponics" comes from the ancient Greek terms "hydro" (water) and "ponics" (work). In hydroponics, plants can establish their roots in a growth media and obtain the nutrients they need from a nutrient solution containing water. Really, there is no soil and no mess! With hydroponics, it is possible to grow plants indoors year-round, regardless of the weather.

Yet, contemporary hydroponics did not arise until the nineteenth century. Julius von Sachs, a German botanist, conducted experiments in 1842 to demonstrate that plants may grow in nutrient-rich water without soil. In the 1930s, scientists began to design commercially viable hydroponic systems, and the technique gained popularity in Europe and the United States.

NASA began experimenting with hydroponic systems to grow plants in space in the 1960s. Urban farmers and hobbyists who wished to cultivate fresh vegetables in small places also adopted the technology. In the 1990s, hydroponics grew in popularity in Asia, particularly Japan, where space was at a premium and farmers sought innovative methods to cultivate food.

Currently, hydroponics is utilized in commercial agriculture, as well as in home gardening and urban farming, across the globe. It has the ability to generate great yields of fresh produce in a small area, while requiring less water and fertilizer than conventional agricultural methods.

Hydroponics is a method of growing plants without soil using mineral nutrient solutions dissolved in water. Using this technology, plants can be cultivated indoors and outdoors, in greenhouses and other places with specialized design. Hydroponics is most frequently used to cultivate vegetables, herbs, fruits, and flowers, but it can also be used to cultivate a number of other plant types.

Without the requirement for soil, hydroponics provides plants with the basic nutrients required for growth, such as nitrogen, phosphorous, potassium, calcium, magnesium, and iron, as well as trace elements such as boron, manganese, and zinc. Typically, plants are cultivated in a substrate or medium, such as gravel, perlite, rockwool, vermiculite, coir, clay pebbles, or even air, to offer the plant roots a place to anchor and absorb the nutrient solution.

A hydroponic system consists of a nutrient reservoir, a delivery system, and a growing container; this system delivers nutrient solutions to the plant roots. Depending on the type of system being utilized, the hydroponic system may be operated manually or automatically. Typically, fertilizer solutions are administered to plants by pump, drip system, or flood and drain system.

Hydroponics is an economical and sustainable method of plant cultivation since it uses less water, fertilizer, and space than soil-based gardening. In addition, hydroponics can be used to cultivate plants in regions where soil is not available, such as deserts, rooftops, and buildings, which creates new opportunities for urban agriculture and food production.

Hydroponics provides a favorable environment for plant growth, resulting in better yields than soil-based cultivation. Hydroponic systems result in faster plant growth, greater flower or fruit production, and more frequent harvesting.

- The fundamental advantage of hydroponic cultivation is that it generates higher-quality food than conventional soil cultivation. Because hydroponic plants are not limited by the availability of nutrients in the soil, they are able to absorb nutrients more efficiently. This results in fruits and vegetables that are larger, more nutritious, and free of soil-borne diseases and pests. In addition, hydroponic plants typically grow quicker than plants grown on soil, resulting in a greater yield.

- Because hydroponic systems use a closed-loop system, water is not wasted and is reused. This is advantageous for regions with limited water resources.
- In hydroponic systems, nutrients are given directly to plant roots, resulting in increased nutrient efficiency. This permits plants to absorb more accessible nutrients, resulting in healthier, more productive plants.
- Hydroponic systems can lessen the risk of introducing soil-borne pests and diseases because they do not require soil.
- Hydroponic systems may be set up in far less space than soil-based growth, making them perfect for urban gardeners with limited space.
- As a result of optimal growing circumstances, plants grown in hydroponic systems tend to grow quicker than those cultivated on soil. This can lead to higher yields in less time.
- The controlled atmosphere of a hydroponic system enables for year-round cultivation, even in regions with frigid winters.

- Plants produced in hydroponic systems typically have more strong tastes and higher vitamin and mineral concentrations than plants cultivated in soil.
- Hydroponic systems offer an unfavorable environment for pests and diseases, hence minimizing the need for chemical pest and disease control.
- Hydroponic methods use typically less energy, water, and fertilizer than soil-based cultivation, resulting in cheaper production costs.
- Allows for greater control over the growing environment by facilitating a microclimate. This includes the capacity to modify the plants' temperature, humidity, and light levels. In addition, in hydroponic farming, the nutrient solution is easily accessible to the roots of the plants, allowing for optimal plant growth and nourishment.
- Improved pH control: Hydroponic systems allow for more precise control over the pH balance of the nutrient solution, ensuring optimal growth conditions.
- This gardening technique Is advantageous since it eliminates the requirement for soil, allowing plants to be grown in any area with minimal space. Because to the small size of hydroponic gardens, they may be put up

indoors or outdoors and are easily transportable.

The nutrient-rich water solutions used in hydroponic farming are adjusted to the unique needs of each plant, supplying them with all the minerals and nutrients they require to flourish. This eliminates the need for laborious and time-consuming soil fertilization. Moreover, hydroponic plants recycle the water they use, resulting in less water waste than traditional gardening. In comparison to traditional gardening, hydroponic gardens are highly efficient and may generate a significant output of plants in a small area. The absence of soil also decreases the risk of pests, illnesses, and weeds, which can be difficult to control in conventional gardens.

- as plants can be provided with the exact nutrients they need at the exact time they need them. Additionally, hydroponics allows for greater control over the environment, making it possible to optimize conditions such as temperature, humidity, and light. This allows for plants to grow faster and more efficiently than they would in soil. Furthermore, hydroponics can be used to grow plants in places where soil is not available, such as urban areas or areas with poor soil quality. Finally, hydroponics is a great way to conserve resources, as it requires less water and fertilizer than traditional soil-based cultivation.

- Hydroponic gardening does not require the use of pesticides or herbicides, as the growing environment can be carefully controlled to ensure the plants are not exposed to any pests or disease.

- Hydroponics is regarded to be an environmentally beneficial method of growing. It involves growing plants without soil, relying instead on a nutrient-rich fluid to provide the plants with the vital nutrients they require to flourish. This gardening technique removes the need for pesticides and other hazardous chemicals and minimizes the quantity of water required to produce plants. Moreover, hydroponics can be utilized to cultivate plants in regions without soil, such as rooftops, greenhouses, and urban environments.

- Hydroponic systems provide a high degree of seasonal predictability. Regardless of the season, plants cultivated in a hydroponic system can be harvested year-round. This is because hydroponic systems may be tailored to offer the optimal temperature, light, humidity, and fertilizer levels for plant development. This lets growers to obtain a yield that is more constant and predictable than traditional soil-based cultivation. Moreover, hydroponic systems can be structured to improve production by taking advantage of seasonal weather fluctuations. For instance, a hydroponic system can be built to boost plant growth and output by taking advantage of summer's warmer temperatures.

- Last, but not least...it's simple!

2

Equipment for Getting Started

What are hydroponics' six requirements?

The six necessities are light, air, water, nutrition, space, and heat. Hydroponic cultivation can occur both indoors and outdoors. In either environment, plants require five to six hours of light each day, access to electricity, and a level, wind-free location.

Water: Irrigation System

In general, hydroponic irrigation systems use drip watering with soilless growing media such as sand, rock wool, or coco-coir. The drip systems feed water to the media by distribution tubing and online barbed drip emitters. A hydroponic drip system is a sort of hydroponic gardening technique that use a network of plastic tubing to provide nutrient solution to the plant roots. Each plant in the system receives the nutrient solution through a drip line that is connected to the main nutrient reservoir. The plant's roots then absorb the nutritional solution, allowing the plant to develop and flourish. Home gardeners use hydroponic drip systems because they are simple to install and maintain and require minimum space.

Drip hydroponics come in a variety of sizes and styles. There are small, counter-top systems ideal for home gardeners, as well as large-scale drip hydroponic systems for commercial farming.

If you are interested in installing your own hydroponic drip system, you will need the following:

Containers

You will need a container to store your plant and water reservoir. The container size depends depend on how many plants you choose to cultivate.

This is the medium in which the plant will be cultivated.
- ➢ Plastic Buckets
  Plastic buckets are lightweight, long-lasting, and simple to use. After filling the buckets with a growing medium such as perlite or coco coir, the plants can be placed inside. The pump will be controlled by the timer, delivering a consistent stream of nutrient-rich water to the plants. The water will drop down into the growing media, supplying nutrients to the plants.
- ➢ Fabric Pots

Fabric pots are an ideal choice for a hydroponic drip system because they provide excellent drainage and allow for easy access to the roots of the plants. Fabric pots are also lightweight and easy to move, making them perfect for growing in a small space. The fabric also helps to keep the roots of the plants aerated, which is essential for healthy growth.

➤ Ebb and Flow Systems

A hydroponic ebb and flow system, also known as a flood and drain system, is a hydroponic method of growing plants in which nutrient-rich water is pumped from a reservoir up to the roots of the plants and then allowed to drain back into the reservoir. A cycle is the process of flooding and draining the root zone of plants. The cycle is usually repeated multiple times per day, and the frequency can be varied to match the needs of the plants. This technique is an efficient way of feeding plants the nutrients they require to develop and thrive.

➤ Flood Tables

The flood table is usually lined with a material such as plastic or clay pebbles to allow the roots of the plants to come in contact with the nutrient solution.

➤ AeroponicSystems

Aeroponic systems are a type of hydroponic system that use air and mist to deliver nutrients to the root zone of plants. In an aeroponic system, the roots of the plants are suspended in the air and misted with a nutrient solution. This method of hydroponic gardening is often considered to be one of the most efficient and effective ways to grow plants.

➢ NFT Systems

A hydroponic drip system, also known as a nutrient film technique (NFT) system, is a hydroponic method of growing plants in which a very shallow stream of water containing all the necessary nutrients required for plant growth is continuously recirculated past the bare roots of plants in a watertight gully. The gully is slightly inclined, so that the nutrient solution flows down the length of the gully and is then pumped back to the top. This system is often used for growing leafy greens and herbs.

➢ Self-Watering Containers A hydroponic drip system is a type of hydroponic gardening method that uses a network of tubes and pumps to deliver nutrient-rich water directly to the roots of plants. The water is delivered in a controlled, consistent drip, allowing the plants to absorb the nutrients they need. This type of system is often used in self-watering containers, which are designed to provide a steady supply of water without the need for manual watering. Self-watering containers are great for those who don't have the time or energy to tend to their plants regularly.

➢ PVC Pipes to deliver a nutrient-rich solution to the plant's roots. The nutrient solution is delivered in a continuous drip, which is regulated by a timer. The nutrient solution is typically delivered to the roots of the plants via a drip line, which is inserted into the medium (such as rockwool, coco coir, or clay pebbles). The nutrient solution is then absorbed by the medium and delivered to the roots of the plants. The PVC pipes are used to connect the nutrient solution reservoir to the drip lines.

Growing Media

Vermiculite, Rockwool, perlite, grow stones, and coco coir are common growing media.

- ➢ Vermiculite is a mineral that is often used in soil-based gardening to help retain moisture and provide aeration to the soil. It is not necessary in a hydroponic drip system, as the plants are grown in a soilless medium such as perlite, coco coir, or rockwool, which provide the necessary moisture and aeration for the plants.
- ➢ Rockwool is manufactured from spun basaltic rock and is highly absorbent, making it perfect for hydroponic farming. In addition to being lightweight, rockwool may be easily moved and rearranged when necessary. In addition, it is highly resistant to fungi and bacteria, which makes it an excellent option for hydroponic systems.
- ➢ Perlite is a type of volcanic glass that is commonly used in hydroponic systems as a growing medium. It is lightweight, sterile, and has good water retention, making it ideal for use in hydroponic

systems. Perlite is also an inert material, meaning it does not affect the pH of the nutrient solution.

- ➢ Grow stones are a type of medium used in hydroponic drip systems. They are made from expanded clay pellets, which are lightweight and porous. The stones provide support for the plants' roots and allow for oxygen and water to penetrate them. The stones also help to retain moisture, which is important for successful hydroponic gardening.
- ➢ Coco coir is a great medium for hydroponics because it is lightweight, has great water retention and aeration properties, and is a renewable resource. The coco coir is mixed with a nutrient solution and then pumped through a drip system to the plants. This system allows for a steady supply of nutrients to the plants, which helps them to grow quickly and healthily.

Nutrition Solution

A nutrition solution — To feed your plant, you will need a nutrient solution. You can either create your own organic nutrient or purchase one on the market. In hydroponics, what nutritional solution is used?

Nitrogen, phosphorus, and potassium are the three primary macronutrients required by all hydroponically cultivated plants. Micronutrients such as calcium, magnesium, sulfur, iron, manganese, copper, zinc, molybdenum, boron, and chlorine are also required by all plants. Is it possible to manufacture my own hydroponic nutrient solution?

While some sources may advise you to only use fertilizers created for hydroponic systems, the University of Florida IFAS Extension reports that it is not only possible but also simple to create your own formula from widely accessible components.

Premade solutions are often more expensive than homemade alternatives, but they might be more convenient and user-friendly. Premade solutions are usually designed to give the proper nutrients for your plants and come with instructions on how to utilize them. They frequently include a timer or other tools to help automate the procedure.

Handmade solutions are typically less expensive than prefabricated ones, but they take more time and work to construct and maintain. You will need to measure out the exact amount of nutrients and, if necessary, alter the pH of the solution. You will also need to monitor the solution on a frequent basis to ensure that it is being used properly. Because you are making the solution from scratch, you must be mindful of any potential hazards linked with the nutrients you are utilizing.

Pump - The pump is usually an electric submersible pump or a diaphragm pump that is connected to the reservoir and the drip system. The pump must be strong enough to move the nutrient solution up to the plants, and it must be able to maintain a constant flow rate. An air stone is used to prevent the nutrient solution from becoming stagnant by aerating it.

Putting up a tiny drip system is straightforward and may be accomplished in a few steps:

Pick a position for your drip system that receives ample sunshine or grow light and has adequate ventilation. If you intend to utilize any fan for ventilation in your hydroponic grow rooms, you should review the following procedures:

> ➤ The reservoir is where the water and fertilizers are stored. It is essential to choose a reservoir large enough to accommodate the amount of plants you intend to cultivate. Also, you will need to drill holes for the plants in the reservoir.
> ➤ Build your grow space. This can be anything from a simple plastic tray to a complicated PVC drip system.
> ➤ Fill the reservoir with water and nutrients; when filling the reservoir, use filtered or distilled water. Moreover, you must add a nutrition solution to the water.
> ➤ Fill the grow area with an inert growing medium - The plant will be grown in the growing medium. Hydroton clay balls and perlite are examples of such items. Put it in the growth area and ensure it is wet.
> ➤ Once the grow medium is in place, you can plant your seeds or seedlings. Ensure that they are

planted deep enough to be submerged in the nutritional solution.

- ➢ The pump is used to circulate water and nutrients throughout the system. It is essential to select a pump of the appropriate size for your system.
- ➢ Set a timer to activate and deactivate the pump as needed.
- ➢ Attach the tubing - After installing the pump, you must connect it to the grow area using tubing. Food-grade and toxin-free tubing should be utilized.
- ➢ Add an air stone - The air stone is used to prevent the nutrient solution from becoming stagnant by aerating it. Switch on the pump and observe the plant's growth!
- ➢ Closely monitor the system and ensure that the plants receive sufficient water and nutrients.

Grow Lights

Hydroponic grow lights are specialized lighting systems designed to provide artificial light for hydroponic-grown plants. Without soil, hydroponic systems involve the cultivation of plants in water or nutrient-rich solutions.

The importance of hydroponic grow lights stems from the fact that they supply the light spectrum, intensity, and duration required for different phases of plant growth. They can be used as a supplement to natural light or as the sole source of illumination for indoor hydroponic gardening.

LED grow lights, high-intensity discharge (HID) grow lights, and fluorescent grow lights are all available as hydroponic grow lights. The choice of grow light will rely on variables such as the size of the growing area, the type of plants being cultivated, and the available budget.

LED grow lights are prevalent because they are energy-efficient, durable, and can emit a complete spectrum of light for plant growth. HID grow lights are also widely employed since their strong light output makes them excellent for wider growing spaces. Fluorescent grow lights are less expensive and appropriate for small to medium-sized growing spaces.

While choosing hydroponic grow lights, it is essential to examine the type of plants being produced, their growth stage, the size of the growing space, and the budget. To achieve optimal plant growth and yield, it is also crucial to evaluate the power output, spectrum, and endurance of the grow lights.

Meters

Hydroponic meters are instruments used to measure various hydroponic system parameters. These meters are necessary for ensuring that the nutrient levels in a hydroponic system are adequate for plant growth. Examples of typical hydroponic meters include:

- The meter that measures the acidity or alkalinity of nutritional solutions. Most hydroponic plants thrive with a pH range between 5.5 and 6.5.

- The used to measure the concentration of dissolved salts in the nutrition solution. This indicates the levels of nutrients in the solution.
- The meter that measures the total amount of dissolved solids in the nutrition solution. This comprises both necessary nutrients and other dissolving substances.
- The meter used to determine the temperature of the nutrient solution. The optimal temperature for the majority of hydroponic plants is between 68 and 72 degrees Fahrenheit (20 and 22 degrees Celsius).
- The meter that measures the amount of available light for plants. This is essential since it helps to calculate the right illumination requirements for various plant species.

By routinely monitoring these metrics, hydroponic farmers may guarantee that their plants receive the proper levels of nutrients, light, and other environmental elements required for optimal growth.

Pest Management Equipment

Products and equipment for hydroponic pest management include a number of instruments and items meant to assist producers in managing pests in hydroponic systems. Here are several examples:

Beneficial Insects: To combat pests, predatory insects like ladybugs, lacewings, and praying mantises can be put into the hydroponic system. The following are examples of common beneficial insects employed in hydroponic pest management:

- Ladybugs are a popular choice for pest control in hydroponics since they feed on aphids, whiteflies, and other soft-bodied pests.
- Lacewings are a popular choice since they feed on aphids, spider mites, and other pests with fragile bodies. In addition, they lay their eggs on leaves, where their larvae will continue to feast on pests.
- Predatory mites: Predatory mites can effectively manage populations of spider mites and other tiny pests by feeding on them.

- Parasitic wasps lay eggs in the bodies of nuisance insects, which hatch and eat the host from the inside out. However, they may not be acceptable for all hydroponic systems despite their effectiveness against insect populations.

It is essential to select the appropriate beneficial insect for the specific pests you are attempting to manage and to ensure that your hydroponic system is conducive to their survival. Beneficial insects can be obtained from reliable vendors and introduced into the hydroponic system at the proper time.

While beneficial insects may not always be adequate to control pest numbers on their own, it is also crucial to monitor the pest population regularly and take action as necessary.

Neem Oil is a pesticide made from the neem tree. It is effective against a variety of pests, including spider mites, whiteflies, and aphids. Here are some tips for utilizing neem oil for insect control in hydroponics:

- Neem oil can be fairly potent, therefore it is essential to dilute it prior to using it in your hydroponic system. Combine 1 gallon of water with 1-2 tablespoons of neem oil.
- Hydroponic plants are cultivated without soil, thus the neem oil must be applied directly to the plant's roots. Put the diluted neem oil to the hydroponic system's reservoir and allow it to circulate.
- Neem oil is efficient at repelling and inhibiting the growth of numerous pests, but it is not a foolproof treatment. Be on the lookout for symptoms of pest damage on your plants, and be prepared to take further precautions if necessary.

- Neem oil can be used as a prophylactic approach to prevent insect infestations from occurring in the first place. Adding diluted neem oil to your hydroponic system on a regular basis can prevent pest infestations.

Pyrethrin is generated from the chrysanthemum flower and is a botanical pesticide. It is deemed safe for use in hydroponic systems and is effective against a broad range of pests. Pyrethrins target the insect's nerve system, resulting in paralysis and death. They are efficient against numerous pests, such as aphids, spider mites, whiteflies, and thrips.

When utilizing pyrethrins for pest control in hydroponics, it is essential to follow the manufacturer's recommendations precisely. Pyrethrins are frequently sold as a concentrate that must be diluted with water prior to application. To administer pyrethrins to the plants, you can use a hand sprayer or a fogger.

When used as prescribed, pyrethrins are generally harmless for humans and animals, but it is still vital to take precautions when handling them. Use gloves and eye protection, and avoid inhaling the spray mist. Use pyrethrins sparingly and only when absolutely necessary, as they can be detrimental to beneficial insects such as bees and ladybugs. Consider use insecticidal soap and neem oil as part of an integrated pest management strategy.

Insecticidal Soap: Insecticidal soap is an alternative with low toxicity for pest control in hydroponic systems. It kills insects by damaging the cell membranes of their bodies. This form of insecticide is composed of natural, non-toxic components, such as plant or animal fatty acids. Insecticidal soap kills insects by breaking their cell membranes, causing dehydration and death.

To effectively utilize insecticidal soap in hydroponic systems, it is essential to adhere to the manufacturer's instructions. It is typically diluted with water and sprayed directly onto the damaged plants. It is essential to cover all plant surfaces, especially the undersides of leaves, where pests frequently lurk.

Insecticidal soap is generally acceptable for use in hydroponic systems and does not leave toxic residues that can harm plants or taint water. It is essential to remember, however, that insecticidal soap is not effective against all types of pests and may need to be used in conjunction with other pest control methods, such as physical barriers or biological controls.

Also, it is vital to exercise caution while using insecticidal soap, as it can be detrimental to beneficial insects such as bees and ladybugs, which assist to naturally decrease pest populations. So, it is advisable to use insecticidal soap as a last resort and only when all other pest control methods have failed.

Sticky traps are a useful tool for monitoring and controlling flying insects such as thrips, whiteflies, and fungus gnats. To efficiently employ sticky traps in a hydroponic system, it is necessary to adhere to the following guidelines:

Identify the type of insect. Various colors of sticky traps attract different types of bugs. Whiteflies, for instance, are attracted to yellow sticky traps, but fungus gnats are drawn to blue or purple sticky traps. Determine which bug is creating the issue in your hydroponic system and select the right color of sticky traps.

Sticky traps should be properly positioned near the plants, but not right on top of them. The traps should be hung at a height where they are most likely to catch the pests, such as at the same level as the plant tops.

➤ Regularly inspect the traps: Inspect the sticky traps on a regular basis to see whether they have captured any bugs. If the traps are full, they must be replaced.

➤ Sticky traps should be utilized as part of an integrated pest management approach, alongside other methods such as biological controls, insecticidal soaps, and neem oil.

Sticky traps can be an effective method for pest management in hydroponic systems. By combining them with other pest management strategies, hydroponic farmers can protect their plants from hazardous pests and maintain their health.

UV Sterilizers: UV sterilizers can be used to manage infections and algae in hydroponic systems. A UV sterilizer can be a useful tool for pest control in hydroponic systems. UV sterilization kills or sterilizes pathogens, such as viruses, bacteria, and fungi, as well as insect eggs and larvae, using ultraviolet radiation. This can reduce the need for chemical pesticides in hydroponic systems by preventing the spread of disease and pests.

When utilizing a UV sterilizer in a hydroponic system, it is essential to verify that the water is flowing smoothly through the sterilizer and is free of debris. The efficacy of the sterilizer can be affected by variables such as water temperature, pH, and dissolved particles; therefore, it is essential to periodically monitor these parameters. UV sterilizers can be successful at killing diseases and pests, although they may not be effective against all types of pests. In some instances, physical barriers or biological control strategies may be required in addition to UV sterilization.

Overall, a UV sterilizer can be a beneficial tool for managing pests in a hydroponic system, but it must be used in conjunction with other pest management strategies and water quality and flow must be monitored on a regular basis.

Water filters can help remove pollutants and pathogens from the water used in a hydroponic system, hence minimizing the danger of pest infestations. Water filters can be a useful tool for hydroponic pest control, since they can remove dangerous microbes and pests from the hydroponic system's water. Here are several applications of water filters in hydroponic pest management:

Water filters may physically trap and remove larger pests and debris from the water. This may include algae, plant material, and insect larvae.

Some forms of water filters, such as biofilters, can assist in the cultivation of beneficial bacteria that can compete with and suppress detrimental microbes and pests.

Chemical filtration: Certain water filters can also remove dangerous chemicals and contaminants from the water, so aiding in the prevention of pests and diseases in hydroponic systems.

Water filters can be a valuable tool in hydroponic pest management, but it is crucial to choose the proper type of filter for your specific needs and to maintain and clean the filter on a regular basis to ensure its efficacy.

PH meters are required for maintaining the proper pH levels in a hydroponic system. Appropriate pH levels encourage healthy plant growth and may also discourage pests. pH meters are crucial for hydroponic pest management because they help to guarantee that the nutrient solution is at the ideal pH level for optimal plant growth and to prevent pest infestations.

In hydroponic systems with an inappropriate pH level, pests such as spider mites, aphids, and whiteflies may flourish. These pests can cause plant damage and productivity reduction. Growers can monitor the pH level of their nutrient solution with pH meters and make modifications as necessary.

The optimal pH range for hydroponic fertilizer solutions is between 5.5 and 6.5. This range is appropriate for plant absorption of important nutrients and aids in the prevention of pest infestations. By frequently testing the fertilizer solution with a pH meter, farmers may verify that the pH is within this range.

Adding an acidic solution, such as vinegar or citric acid, can lower the pH if it is too high. Adding an alkaline solution such as baking soda or potassium hydroxide might raise the pH if it is too low. However, caution must be exercised when adjusting the pH, as abrupt fluctuations might shock the plants.

PH meters are essential for hydroponic pest management because they enable producers to maintain the optimal pH range for their nutrient solution, thereby preventing pest infestations and encouraging healthy plant growth.

Nutrient meters can be utilized to monitor the nutrient levels in a hydroponic system. Appropriate nutrition levels can aid in promoting healthy plant development and repelling pests. Hydroponic gardeners require nutrient meters to maintain optimum nutrient levels in their systems. These meters measure the amounts of nutrients such as nitrogen, phosphorous, and potassium in the hydroponic solution, ensuring that the plants receive the nutrients necessary for healthy growth.

Unfortunately, nutrient meters in hydroponic systems do not immediately address pest management. Pest management in hydroponics consists of monitoring plants for signs of pests, applying preventative measures such as introducing beneficial insects or utilizing natural pest control products, and treating pests with the proper pesticides or fungicides.

Thus, nutrition meters can indirectly aid in pest control by ensuring that plants are healthy and less vulnerable to assault. Healthy plants are less likely to attract pests and are better equipped to defend themselves against potential threats.

Despite the fact that nutrient meters are not directly related to pest management in hydroponics, they can indirectly aid in maintaining healthy plants and reducing the danger of insect infestations.

Air Filters: Air filters can assist in removing dust, mold spores, and other airborne pathogens from a hydroponic system's air, hence lowering the likelihood of pest infestations. In hydroponic systems, air filters can play a vital role in pest management. The filter can assist prevent pests from entering the growing area by capturing them. In addition, air filters can eliminate particle matter, thereby preventing the transmission of disease and fungal spores.

While choosing an air filter for your hydroponic system, it is essential to examine the filter's size in relation to your growing space. You should also select a filter with a MERV (minimal efficiency reporting value) rating high enough to adequately catch the size of the pests you wish to prevent from entering the area. Also, routine cleaning of the air filter is necessary to maintain its continued efficiency. Maintenance includes regular filter cleaning or replacement, depending on the type of filter being utilized. While air filters can be an efficient tool for pest management in hydroponics, they should not be relied on as the main technique. A complete plan for integrated pest management should be devised, incorporating a variety of measures for preventing and controlling pests in the growing region.

3

Hydroponic Growing Systems

There are various sorts of hydroponic systems, each with its own set of benefits and drawbacks. When selecting a system, consider aspects such as available space, the sort of plants you want to cultivate, your budget, and your level of skill.

Deep Water Culture (DWC) or Floating Rafts

This system involves suspending plants in a nutrient-rich water solution, with their roots submerged in the water. Hydroponic deep water culture is a type of hydroponic system that involves suspending plant roots in a nutrient-rich water solution. The plants are placed in net pots or other containers that are suspended over a tank or reservoir filled with aerated water.

Deep water culture is the most simple type of hydroponic system to build and maintain at home.

Deep water culture (DWC) is often considered an easy hydroponic system for beginners for several reasons:

- Simple setup: DWC systems typically have a simple setup with few components, making them easy to assemble and maintain. The system consists of a reservoir, an air pump, an air stone, and a net pot for the plant.
- Low cost: DWC systems can be built using inexpensive materials such as plastic buckets, tubing, and air stones. This makes them a cost-effective option for beginners who want to try hydroponics without investing a lot of money upfront.
- Minimal maintenance: DWC systems require minimal maintenance, as the plants are suspended in water and receive all of their nutrients directly from the nutrient-rich water. This eliminates the need for soil, fertilizers, and frequent watering.

- Fast growth: Plants grown in DWC systems often experience rapid growth due to the availability of nutrients and oxygen in the water.
- Easy to monitor: DWC systems are easy to monitor, as the nutrient solution can be easily checked for pH and nutrient levels using a simple testing kit.

The simplicity, low cost, minimal maintenance, fast growth, and easy monitoring make deep water culture an attractive option for beginners who want to try hydroponics.

The roots of the plants are allowed to dangle down into the water, where they absorb nutrients and oxygen directly from the solution. The water in the reservoir is typically oxygenated using an air pump or other method to ensure that the roots have a steady supply of oxygen.

Deep water culture (DWC) systems are popular for growing plants like lettuce, herbs, and other leafy greens, but can also be used for growing larger plants like tomatoes or cucumbers.

One advantage of DWC systems is that they are relatively simple and inexpensive to set up and maintain. They also allow for easy monitoring of nutrient levels and pH, and can be scaled up or down depending on the needs of the grower.

However, DWC systems require careful attention to water quality and temperature, as well as proper maintenance of equipment like pumps and aerators. Additionally, because the plants rely solely on the water for nutrients, any imbalances or deficiencies in the nutrient solution can quickly lead to plant health problems.

Drip Irrigation

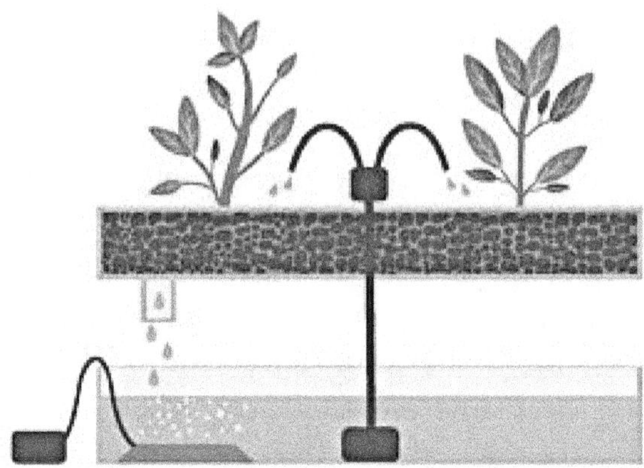

This system involves dripping nutrient-rich water solution directly onto the roots of the plants.

In this system, water and nutrients are delivered directly to the roots of the plants through small tubes or drippers.

The process involves placing the plants in a growing medium such as rockwool or coco coir, and then running a series of tubes or drippers through the growing medium. These tubes or drippers are connected to a reservoir of nutrient-rich water that is pumped into the system and dripped onto the roots of the plants.

The advantage of hydroponic drip irrigation is that it allows for precise control of the amount of water and nutrients delivered to each plant. This can result in faster growth, higher yields, and better quality produce. Additionally, since the water is delivered directly to the roots, there is less waste and less chance of overwatering or underwatering the plants.

Nutrient Film Technique (NFT)

Nutrition film technique (NFT) hydroponic system is one of the most prevalent and commonly utilized types of hydroponic systems. You can have a healthy NFT system up and operating quickly with just a little amount of consideration and effort. NFT systems are very efficient and straightforward to implement.

The Nutrient Film Technique, often known as NFT, is a type of hydroponic system that delivers nutrients to plants via a nutrient-enriched water film that is extremely thin. Continuous absorption of the nutrient solution by the plant's roots provides the plant with everything necessary for its further development.

The water is circulated throughout the system by means of a series of smaller channels, each of which is contained by a screen or net. The plants' root systems extend into the channels, where they are saturated with nutrient-rich water. NFT systems are highly efficient and may be set up with minimal effort. In addition to this, NFT systems are frequently very well ventilated, which is an additional vital aspect of plant development.

Using an NFT hydroponic system provides a variety of significant benefits, including the following: In the following paragraphs, each of these benefits will be analyzed in greater detail.

Regarding the utilization of water and nutrients, NFT systems are highly efficient.

Since the roots of the plants are regularly bathed in a thin layer of nutrient-rich water, there is a negligible amount of water and nutrient loss. This results in minimal water and nutrient loss. NFT systems are therefore a viable choice for farmers who wish to reduce the quantity of water and fertilizers used in their operations.

In terms of installation and maintenance, NFT hydroponic systems are among the most user-friendly compared to other types of hydroponic systems. Farmers that do not want to spend a great deal of time setting up and maintaining their systems may find NFT systems beneficial.

Adding additional channels or making modifications to the existing channels is all that is required to expand an NFT system. Due to this adaptability, NFT systems are a terrific choice for farmers who wish to experiment with various development techniques or who like to expand or contract their firm based on the circumstances.

The roots of the plant are continuously coated with a thin layer of nutrient-rich water, which provides them with everything they need to develop properly and enables them to continue growing. Additionally, NFT systems are frequently well-aerated, which is another factor that plays a significant influence in plant growth.

The following are essential NFT system components:

- A nutrient reservoir is the location where you will store the created nutrition solution.
- There is a pump that circulates the nutritional solution throughout the system.
- Grow channels are the channels into which the plant's roots will descend once the plant is established. They must have a slope so that water can flow through them more freely.
- A timer is required since it is utilized to turn on and off the pump at predefined intervals.
- The roots of your garden plants can be aerated with the aid of an air pump and an air stone.

Determine where your NFT system will be installed. The area must contain grow channels that have been constructed or acquired. The gradient of the channels must be modified so that water can flow through them unimpeded.

Insert the nutrition reservoir and ensure that it is properly connected to the pump. The pump will be controlled by the timer, which will switch it on and off at predetermined intervals.

Place an air pump and an air stone within the reservoir to aerate the water. This will ensure that the plant roots receive adequate ventilation and prevent root rot.

If you follow these four steps, you will be able to get a basic NFT system operational. After completing the initial configuration of your NFT system, you can proceed to adding plants.

Aeroponics

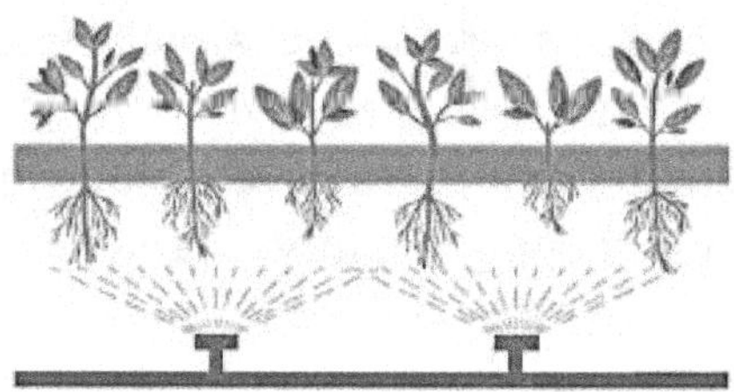

This system involves suspending plants in a chamber and misting the roots with nutrient-rich water solution. An aeroponic hydroponic system is a type of hydroponic system that uses mist or fog to deliver nutrients and water directly to the roots of plants. In an aeroponic system, plants are grown in a container with their roots suspended in the air, and nutrient-rich water is sprayed onto the roots in a fine mist or fog. This allows the plants to absorb nutrients and water directly through their roots, without the need for soil.

Aeroponic systems are highly efficient and can produce larger yields than traditional soil-based gardening methods. They are also highly customizable and can be used to grow a wide variety of plants, including vegetables, herbs, and flowers.

One of the key advantages of aeroponic systems is that they use less water than traditional gardening methods, making them an ideal choice for areas with water shortages or where water is expensive. They also require less space than traditional gardening methods, making them ideal for urban environments or small spaces.

However, aeroponic systems can be more difficult to set up and maintain than other types of hydroponic systems, as they require more specialized equipment and monitoring. They are also more sensitive to environmental changes, such as temperature and humidity, and require a more precise balance of nutrients and water to ensure optimal plant growth.

Wicking

Wicking is one of the simplest types of hydroponic systems. In this system, the plant is placed in an inert growing medium like perlite or coconut coir, and a wick is used to draw the nutrient solution from the reservoir to the plant's roots.

The wick can be made of any absorbent material like cotton, nylon, or felt. One end of the wick is placed in the nutrient solution, and the other end is placed in contact with the growing medium. The wick transports the nutrient solution from the reservoir to the roots through capillary action.

Wicking systems are low-maintenance and low-cost, making them a popular choice for beginners. However, they are not suitable for large plants or plants with high nutrient requirements since the wick can only transport a limited amount of nutrient solution.

Make sure that you have completely gone through the instructions on how to set up your hydroponics system so that you can put it up in the location that you desire in the most effective manner!

In order to put together this Hydroponics System, you will need at least one bucket that is five gallons in capacity and has a hole in the lid.

You are going to need the following in addition to that:

- Hydroponic medium (such as soil, vermiculite, etc)
- Water
- Nutrients
- Material for wicking
- Plant pots

The construction of a wick hydroponic system consists of the following phases.

1. To begin, you will have to look for an area that is large enough for your hydroponic plants, receives adequate amounts of sunshine, and has adequate lighting. Grow lights that are available for purchase can also be used to offer safe artificial illumination if it is required.
2. Drill four holes into the sides of the bucket you're using for hydroponics, not too far from the bottom. If you drill too deeply into the hydroponic bucket, the growth media will mix with the water, which may quickly ruin your hydroponics system! Therefore be careful not to drill too deeply!
3. Cotton should be chosen for the wick because it is capable of absorbing water and is also permeable enough to allow capillary action. Cotton string should be cut into sections that are approximately six inches longer than the height of your hydroponic bucket. Knot each end of the piece after you have threaded it through one of the drilled holes in a crisscross pattern. This will ensure that the component is secure. Following this process, if there is any excess cotton thread left over, simply clip it off or just leave them for aesthetics; also, it assists in stabilizing hydroponics plants that are being placed within this hydroponics system.

Wicks can be constructed out of a variety of materials including yarn, cloth or rope. The substance might be anything, including wool, cotton, jute, wool, polyurethane, or any of a number of other synthetic materials.

Imagine that you want to use hydroponic plants that were originally cultivated on soil. In such scenario, you don't need to do any more processes; you can just put these hydroponic plants straight into the bucket for hydroponics without any intervening stages. Prepare your hydroponic plants by taking them from the hydroponic pots in which they were growing and removing some of the dirt from around the roots of the hydroponic plants.

4. Place an air stone in the bottom of the hydroponics reservoir, and then position it such that it is in close proximity to the air pump's intake valve. This will ensure that your hydroponic plants receive a steady supply of oxygen throughout the growing process.

5. After placing the air stone in the Hydroponic bucket, pour either hydroponic nutrients or water that has been diluted with hydroponic nutrients into the bottom of the bucket until it completely covers the holes that were bored in Step 1. This will guarantee that the Wick Hydroponics system receives a steady supply of nutrients during its operation!

When inserting your hydroponic plants into the holes, do it carefully and check to see that the roots of the hydroponic plants are in direct touch with the cotton threads. Be sure the bucket contains an appropriate hydroponic media before using it. You may either insert one hydroponic plant per hole or two hydroponic plants per hole, depending on the type of hydroponic plants that you are cultivating; the number of plants that you place in each hole is determined by the type of hydroponic plants that you are cultivating!

Or It is possible to place the plants in the hydroponic medium that is contained in the bucket. Due to the fact that the plants obtain all of the water and nutrients that they require from the media in which they are grown, it is of the utmost importance that the medium be one that both drains and retains moisture. The most common types of growth media used in wicking systems include coco coir chips, vermiculite, coconut fiber, vermiculite.

These growing media are able to effectively wick water, which helps to maintain a moist root zone while also providing sufficient oxygen to the roots. Plants can benefit from the use of growstones. They are able to assist with both water and air. To thrive, plants require an abundance of water as well as air. The majority of wicking systems include the plants being positioned directly within an absorbent medium such as perlite or vermiculite.

6. Take a peek at the Wick Hydroponics system's hydroponic bucket once all of your hydroponically grown plants have been inserted into the system. In the event that the cotton strings have gotten dry, apply additional hydroponic nutrients or water that has been combined with hydroponic nutrients until the medium completely fills the holes that were made in the first step.

That wraps it up!

The wick hydroponics system is well suited for hydroponic plants that do not need for a very extensive root system. This is appropriate for use with fruits like strawberries or tomatoes, as well as vegetables like lettuce, cucumbers, or peas, and herbs like basil and parsley. Essentially, you may cultivate any and all hydroponic plants that are on the smaller side in a wick hydroponics system that is appropriate!

Ebb and flow

Ebb and Flow, also known as Flood and Drain, is one of the popular types of hydroponic systems. In this system, plants are grown in a tray or container filled with a growing medium such as gravel, perlite, or Rockwool. The container is periodically flooded with nutrient-rich water, which is then drained back into the reservoir. Here are the basic steps of an ebb and flow system:

1. The plants are placed in a container filled with a growing medium.
2. The container is flooded with nutrient-rich water from a reservoir.
3. The water is allowed to soak the growing medium for a set amount of time (usually 15-30 minutes).
4. The water is then drained back into the reservoir.
5. The cycle is repeated on a regular schedule, typically several times a day.

Ebb and flow systems are relatively easy to set up and can be used to grow a wide range of plants. They are particularly well-suited to larger plants with deep root systems, such as tomatoes and peppers. However, they do require a bit more maintenance than some other hydroponic systems, as the water and nutrient levels need to be monitored and adjusted regularly.

> A bottle hydroponic system is a simple and inexpensive hydroponic system that you can make using plastic bottles. It's a type of hydroponic system that is suitable for growing small plants such as herbs, lettuce, and small vegetables.

To create a bottle hydroponic system, you will need:

- Plastic bottles (2-liter soda bottles or 20-ounce water bottles work well)
- A sharp knife or scissors
- Hydroponic growing medium (such as perlite, vermiculite, or coconut coir)
- Hydroponic nutrients
- Seeds or seedlings

Here's how to make a bottle hydroponic system:

> Cut the top off the bottle using a sharp knife or scissors. Cut just below the point where the bottle starts to narrow, so you have a wide opening.
> Cut several small holes in the side of the bottle, near the bottom. These holes will serve as drainage holes for excess water.
> Fill the bottom of the bottle with hydroponic growing medium, leaving a small space at the top.
> Add water and hydroponic nutrients to the bottle, following the instructions on the nutrient package. The water should cover the bottom of the growing medium.
> Plant seeds or seedlings in the growing medium, following the instructions for the specific plant you are growing.

> ➤ Place the bottle in a sunny location or under a grow light, and make sure it stays moist by adding water and nutrients as needed.

As the plants grow, you will need to add more water and nutrients to the system. With proper care, a bottle hydroponic system can provide fresh herbs and vegetables year-round.

Vertical Gardens

One type of hydroponic system is the vertical garden.

Vertical gardens are designed to take advantage of vertical space by growing plants on a vertical surface, such as a wall or fence. In a hydroponic vertical garden, plants are typically grown in stacked layers, with water and nutrients circulating through the system to feed the plants.

There are several benefits to using a hydroponic vertical garden system. One of the main advantages is that it allows you to grow a large number of plants in a relatively small space. This makes it ideal for urban gardening, where space is often limited.

Another benefit of hydroponic vertical gardens is that they can be used to grow a wide range of plants, including fruits, vegetables, and herbs. Because the plants are grown in a controlled environment, it is also possible to grow them year-round, regardless of the outdoor climate.

In addition to their practical benefits, hydroponic vertical gardens can also be aesthetically pleasing. They can add a touch of greenery to indoor or outdoor spaces, and can even be used to create living walls that serve as natural air purifiers.

Overall, hydroponic vertical gardens are a versatile and innovative way to grow plants. Whether you are looking to grow your own produce, create a unique decorative feature, or simply explore the world of hydroponic gardening, a vertical garden system may be the perfect solution for you.

Media Beds

Hydroponic systems that use media beds are a popular choice among growers because they are relatively easy to set up and maintain. Media beds typically consist of a container filled with a growing medium, such as perlite, coconut coir, or gravel, and a water reservoir located beneath the bed.

In a media bed hydroponic system, plants are grown in the growing medium rather than soil. The growing medium provides support for the plants' roots and allows them to access water and nutrients from the water reservoir below. The water in the reservoir is typically circulated using a pump, and it may be supplemented with nutrients to ensure that the plants receive everything they need to grow.

One of the benefits of using media beds in hydroponic systems is that they are relatively low-maintenance. Once the system is set up, growers typically only need to monitor the water and nutrient levels and adjust them as needed. Media beds are also versatile and can be used to grow a wide variety of crops, including vegetables, herbs, and fruits.

However, media bed hydroponic systems also have some drawbacks. For example, they can be relatively heavy and may require additional structural support to prevent the growing bed from collapsing. They can also be prone to clogging, particularly if the growing medium used is fine-grained.

Media bed hydroponic systems are a popular choice among growers because of their simplicity and versatility, but they do require careful management to ensure optimal plant growth and health.

4

Planting and Caring

Seeds

One popular medium for starting seeds in hydroponics is stone wool.

Stone wool is made by heating natural rock or mineral fibers until they melt, and then spinning them into long fibers that are formed into mats or cubes. These cubes or mats provide a sterile, porous environment for seeds to germinate and grow roots.

To start seeds in stone wool for hydroponics, follow these steps:

> ➢ Soak the stone wool cubes or mats in pH balanced water for at least an hour. This will help to hydrate the stone wool and ensure that it has a neutral pH.

> ➤ Place one or two seeds in each cube or mat. Make sure to position the seeds in the center of the cube or mat, and then gently push them down into the stone wool.
> ➤ Place the cubes or mats in a warm, dark place, such as a germination chamber or a covered tray. The temperature should be around 70-75°F (21-24°C) for optimal germination.
> ➤ Once the seeds have germinated and started to grow roots, move the cubes or mats to your hydroponic system. Make sure the roots are well-established before transplanting to prevent damage.
> ➤ Maintain the appropriate nutrient solution and pH level for your plants, and monitor their growth closely.

With proper care and attention, seedlings started in stone wool can thrive in a hydroponic system and produce healthy, vigorous plants.

Cuttings

Stone wool is a popular medium for rooting cuttings in hydroponic systems. It is made from melted rock and slag that is spun into fibers, which are then compressed into mats or cubes.

To root cuttings in stone wool, follow these steps:

> ➤ Soak the stone wool cubes or mats in pH-balanced water for at least an hour before use.

- ➤ Take cuttings from healthy plants, making sure to use sharp, sterilized shears.
- ➤ Remove any leaves from the bottom third of the cutting.
- ➤ Make a small hole in the center of the stone wool cube or mat with a pencil or other tool.
- ➤ Insert the cutting into the hole, making sure it is snugly held in place.
- ➤ Mist the cuttings with water to keep them moist.
- ➤ Place the cuttings in a warm, bright location with high humidity, such as a propagator or under a clear plastic dome.
- ➤ Check the cuttings regularly for signs of rooting, such as new growth or resistance when gently tugged.
- ➤ Once the cuttings have rooted, they can be transplanted into a hydroponic system or soil.
- ➤ Stone wool is a good choice for rooting cuttings because it is sterile, pH-neutral, and holds water well. However, it is important to be careful when handling it, as the fibers can irritate the skin, eyes, and lungs. Always wear gloves and a mask when working with stone wool, and dispose of used mats and cubes properly.

Rooting cuttings in a hydroponic cloner is a popular method used by many hydroponic growers to propagate plants. In this method, a hydroponic cloner is used to create a humid environment that encourages the cuttings to form roots.

To root cuttings in a hydroponic cloner, you will need:

Hydroponic cloner: A hydroponic cloner is a device that provides a humid environment for cuttings to root. It usually consists of a reservoir, a pump, and a misting system.

- ➢ Cuttings: Take cuttings from the mother plant using a sharp, clean pair of scissors. The cuttings should be around 4-6 inches long and should have at least two sets of leaves.
- ➢ Rooting hormone: Dip the bottom of the cuttings in a rooting hormone powder or gel to encourage root growth.
- ➢ Water: Fill the hydroponic cloner with water and add any required nutrients according to the instructions.
- ➢ Place the cuttings in the cloner: Place the cuttings in the hydroponic cloner and make sure they are submerged in the water. The misting system will provide moisture to the cuttings and help them to form roots.
- ➢ Wait for the roots to develop: It may take several days for the cuttings to form roots. Check the cloner daily and make sure the water level is maintained. Once the roots have developed, you can transplant the cuttings into a hydroponic system or soil.

Rooting cuttings in a hydroponic cloner is a simple and effective way to propagate plants. With proper care and attention, you can quickly produce new plants and expand your hydroponic garden.

Transplanting

If you have plants that were started in soil and you want to transplant them into a hydroponic system, there are a few things you need to keep in mind.

First, you will need to remove as much of the soil from the roots as possible. This can be done by gently shaking the plant to loosen the soil, or by rinsing the roots with water. Be careful not to damage the roots while doing this.

Once you have removed as much soil as possible, you can then place the plant into your hydroponic system. Make sure the roots are fully submerged in the nutrient solution and that the plant is well supported.

It's also important to note that plants that have been started in soil may take some time to adjust to the new growing conditions. You may need to monitor the plants closely and make adjustments to the nutrient solution as needed to ensure they are getting the right balance of nutrients. With patience and care, however, you can successfully transplant plants from soil into a hydroponic system.

Nutrients

In hydroponic systems, plants obtain nutrients primarily through the solution in which they are grown. The uptake of nutrients by plants in hydroponic systems is a complex process that involves several factors, including the type of nutrient solution used, the pH and temperature of the solution, the species of plant being grown, and the stage of growth of the plant.

Plants in hydroponic systems take up nutrients through their roots, just like in soil-based systems. The nutrient solution in hydroponics is typically composed of water and a mixture of essential nutrients, including nitrogen, phosphorus, potassium, calcium, magnesium, and various micronutrients.

Plants absorb nutrients from the nutrient solution in two ways: passive uptake and active uptake. Passive uptake occurs when nutrients move across the root membrane from areas of high concentration in the solution to areas of low concentration in the root. Active uptake, on the other hand, involves the use of energy by the plant to move nutrients against a concentration gradient, from areas of low concentration in the solution to areas of high concentration in the root.

The uptake of nutrients in hydroponic systems can be influenced by several factors. For example, the pH of the nutrient solution can affect the availability of nutrients to the plant. Most plants grow best in a slightly acidic solution with a pH between 5.5 and 6.5. If the pH of the nutrient solution is too high or too low, some nutrients may become unavailable to the plant, leading to nutrient deficiencies.

Temperature is another factor that can influence nutrient uptake in hydroponic systems. Plants grown in hydroponic systems generally require a higher temperature range than those grown in soil-based systems, typically between 68 and 78 degrees Fahrenheit. At higher temperatures, the solubility of nutrients increases, making them more available to the plant.

Finally, the stage of growth of the plant can also affect nutrient uptake in hydroponic systems. Different nutrients are required at different stages of growth, and the nutrient solution should be adjusted accordingly. For example, plants in the vegetative stage require higher levels of nitrogen, while those in the flowering stage require higher levels of phosphorus and potassium.

Fertlizers

Hydroponic fertilizers are specially formulated fertilizers designed to provide the necessary nutrients to plants grown in hydroponic systems. Hydroponics is a method of growing plants without soil, where the plant roots are placed in a nutrient-rich water solution.

Since hydroponic plants do not have access to soil, they rely entirely on the nutrients added to the water solution. Therefore, hydroponic fertilizers are essential for the growth and health of hydroponic plants. Hydroponic fertilizers are typically composed of the essential nutrients that plants require, including nitrogen, phosphorus, and potassium, as well as other micronutrients such as iron, calcium, and magnesium.

There are many different types of hydroponic fertilizers available, including liquid, powder, and granular formulations. The type of fertilizer used will depend on the specific needs of the plants being grown and the type of hydroponic system being used.

It is important to choose a hydroponic fertilizer that is specifically designed for hydroponic systems, as regular garden fertilizers may contain elements that can be harmful to hydroponic plants or may not contain the necessary nutrients in the correct proportions.

Hydroponic fertilizers are specifically formulated to provide essential nutrients to plants grown in hydroponic systems. These nutrients are dissolved in water and delivered directly to the plant roots, which allows for better nutrient uptake and faster growth.

There are several types of hydroponic fertilizers, including:

- ➢ Complete Nutrient Solutions: These are pre-mixed solutions that contain all the necessary macro and micronutrients required for plant growth. They come in two parts, Part A and Part B, which are mixed together to create a complete nutrient solution.

- ➢ Individual Nutrient Solutions: These are single nutrient solutions that provide specific macronutrients or micronutrients that may be lacking in the complete nutrient solution. This allows for more precise control over nutrient levels and can be especially useful in situations where certain nutrients are depleted more quickly.

- ➢ Organic Nutrient Solutions: These are hydroponic fertilizers that are made from natural, organic sources, such as fish emulsion or seaweed extract. They are often preferred by growers who are looking to grow organic produce and want to avoid synthetic fertilizers.

- ➢ Synthetic Nutrient Solutions: These are hydroponic fertilizers that are made from synthetic sources, such as chemical salts. They are often cheaper than organic nutrient solutions but may not be suitable for all plants or growing situations.
- ➢ PH Adjusters: Hydroponic systems require a specific pH range for optimal nutrient uptake, and pH adjusters are used to modify the pH of the nutrient solution. Common pH adjusters include citric acid and potassium hydroxide.
- ➢ Supplements: Hydroponic supplements are used to provide additional nutrients, such as calcium or magnesium, that may be lacking in the nutrient solution. They are often used in conjunction with complete nutrient solutions or individual nutrient solutions.

In hydroponic systems, measuring fertilizer concentration is important to ensure that plants receive the nutrients they need to grow and thrive. One common method of measuring fertilizer concentration is by using an electrical conductivity (EC) meter.

An EC meter measures the electrical conductivity of the nutrient solution in the hydroponic system. This measurement can be used to determine the concentration of dissolved salts, which is an indicator of the nutrient concentration in the solution.

To measure fertilizer concentration using an EC meter, first, you need to calibrate the meter using a calibration solution. Once calibrated, you can place the meter probe into the nutrient solution and take a reading. The reading will give you an EC value, which can be converted into a measure of nutrient concentration using a conversion factor.

It's important to note that different plants have different nutrient requirements, so the optimal fertilizer concentration will vary depending on the type of plant being grown.

The fertilizer concentration may need to be adjusted over time as plants grow and nutrient uptake changes. Regular monitoring of fertilizer concentration using an EC meter can help ensure that plants are getting the nutrients they need to grow and produce healthy yields.

Problems and Solutions

There are several potential issues that can arise when seeding in hydroponics. Here are some common problems and their possible solutions:

Poor germination: If your seeds are not germinating or are germinating poorly, it could be due to inadequate moisture or temperature. Make sure that your growing medium is evenly moist and that the temperature is within the recommended range for your specific crop.

Damping-off: Damping-off is a fungal disease that can affect seedlings in hydroponics. It typically occurs when the growing medium is too wet and there is poor air circulation. To prevent damping-off, make sure that your growing medium is not too wet and that there is adequate air circulation around your seedlings.

Nutrient deficiency: If your seedlings are not growing properly or are showing signs of nutrient deficiency, it could be due to an imbalanced nutrient solution. Make sure that you are providing your plants with the correct balance of nutrients and adjust your nutrient solution as needed.

pH imbalance: The pH of your nutrient solution can also affect seed germination and plant growth. Make sure that your pH is within the recommended range for your specific crop and adjust your nutrient solution as needed.

Pest and disease issues: Just like with traditional gardening, pests and diseases can also be a problem in hydroponics. To prevent these issues, make sure to maintain good sanitation practices, monitor your plants regularly, and treat any issues promptly.

The key to successful hydroponic seeding is to maintain a healthy environment for your plants and to monitor their progress closely. With proper care and attention, you can overcome many of the common issues that arise during the seeding process in hydroponics.It is still possible for plants grown hydroponically to experience nutrient deficiencies. Here are some common nutrient deficiencies and their symptoms in hydroponic plants:

- Nitrogen Deficiency: Nitrogen is an essential nutrient for plant growth and is necessary for the production of proteins, chlorophyll, and DNA. Plants that are deficient in nitrogen will have pale, yellow leaves that eventually turn brown and wilt. The growth of the plant will also be stunted.

- Phosphorus Deficiency: Phosphorus is important for root growth and the production of flowers and fruits. Plants that are deficient in phosphorus will have dark green leaves that eventually turn purple or red. The leaves may also be smaller than normal, and the plant will produce fewer flowers and fruits.
- Potassium Deficiency: Potassium is necessary for the regulation of water and nutrient uptake in plants, and is important for the production of sugars and starches. Plants that are deficient in potassium will have yellowing and browning on the tips and edges of their leaves. The leaves may also be curled or have a scorched appearance.
- Calcium Deficiency: Calcium is important for cell wall development and overall plant structure. Plants that are deficient in calcium will have distorted or misshapen leaves and stems. The roots may also be stunted, and the plant may be more susceptible to diseases.
- Magnesium Deficiency: Magnesium is essential for the production of chlorophyll, which is necessary for photosynthesis. Plants that are deficient in magnesium will have yellowing leaves that appear to have green veins. The plant may also have stunted growth.

It is important to monitor nutrient levels in hydroponic systems and adjust the nutrient solution as needed to prevent deficiencies. Adding a balanced nutrient solution or a specific nutrient supplement can help address deficiencies and promote healthy plant growth.

Hydroponic systems can be susceptible to various types of pests and diseases. Here are some common hydroponic infestations and ways to control them:

Aphids: These tiny insects can infest hydroponic plants and cause damage by sucking the sap out of the leaves. To control aphids, you can use insecticidal soap, neem oil, or ladybugs.

Spider mites: These pests are common in hydroponic systems and can cause damage by sucking the sap out of the leaves. To control spider mites, you can use a miticide or insecticidal soap.

Fungus gnats: These small flying insects can infest hydroponic systems and cause damage by feeding on the roots. To control fungus gnats, you can use sticky traps or nematodes.

Root rot: This disease is caused by a fungal infection and can cause damage by rotting the roots of the plants. To control root rot, you can use a hydrogen peroxide solution or beneficial bacteria.

Powdery mildew: This fungal disease can cause damage by covering the leaves with a white powdery substance. To control powdery mildew, you can use a fungicide or neem oil.

It's important to maintain good hygiene in your hydroponic system and regularly inspect your plants for signs of infestation or disease. Early detection and control can prevent serious damage to your plants.

5

Maintenance

Hydroponic maintenance involves several tasks that ensure your plants are healthy and growing in the best possible conditions. Here are some key maintenance tasks to keep in mind:

> Check pH and nutrient levels: Regularly check the pH and nutrient levels in your hydroponic system using a pH meter and nutrient testing kit. Adjust these levels as needed to ensure that your plants have the nutrients they need to grow.

> Monitor water levels: Make sure your plants have enough water at all times. Check the water level in your hydroponic system regularly and add more water as needed.

> Clean your system: Keep your hydroponic system clean to prevent the buildup of algae, bacteria, and other contaminants. Clean the reservoir and any

other components regularly using a mild detergent and water.
- ➢ Maintain temperature and humidity: Maintain the appropriate temperature and humidity levels for your plants. Use a thermometer and hygrometer to monitor these levels and adjust them as needed.
- ➢ Check for pests and diseases: Inspect your plants regularly for signs of pests or diseases. If you notice any issues, take action immediately to prevent the problem from spreading.
- ➢ Prune your plants: Regularly prune your plants to remove dead or damaged leaves and encourage new growth.

Managing the nutrient solution is one of the most important aspects of hydroponic gardening. Here are some tips to help you manage your nutrient solution effectively:
- ➢ Monitor the pH: The pH of your nutrient solution is crucial for the health of your plants. Most plants prefer a pH range of 5.5 to 6.5. You should check the pH of your solution regularly and adjust it as needed. pH test strips or a pH meter can be used to check the pH.
- ➢ Check the EC: The electrical conductivity (EC) of your nutrient solution is a measure of the concentration of dissolved salts in the solution. You should check the EC of your solution regularly to ensure that it is within the recommended range for your plants. EC meters are used to measure the EC.

➤ Adjust the nutrient levels: You will need to adjust the nutrient levels in your solution based on the growth stage of your plants. During the vegetative stage, your plants will need more nitrogen, while during the flowering stage, they will need more phosphorus and potassium. You can use hydroponic nutrient solutions that are specifically formulated for different stages of plant growth.

➤ Keep the solution aerated: Your nutrient solution should be aerated to provide oxygen to the roots of your plants. This can be done using an air pump and air stones.

➤ Change the solution regularly: It is important to change your nutrient solution regularly to avoid the buildup of salts and other minerals that can be harmful to your plants. How often you change the solution will depend on the size of your hydroponic system and the growth stage of your plants.

Flushing

Hydroponic flushing is the process of removing excess nutrients and salts from the root zone of plants grown in a hydroponic system. The purpose of flushing is to prevent the buildup of excess nutrients and salts, which can harm plant growth and development.

Flushing is typically done by adding large amounts of clean, pH-balanced water to the hydroponic system. The water is then allowed to circulate through the system for a period of time, usually several hours or overnight. This helps to dissolve and flush out any excess nutrients and salts that may have accumulated in the root zone.

After flushing, the hydroponic system should be allowed to drain completely, and fresh nutrient solution should be added. This helps to ensure that the plants have access to the right balance of nutrients and that the root zone remains healthy.

Flushing is an important part of hydroponic system maintenance and should be done regularly, especially if the nutrient solution is not being changed frequently. Flushing frequency can vary depending on the type of system, plant growth stage, and other factors, so it is important to monitor plants regularly and adjust flushing frequency as needed.

Cleaning

Hydroponic cleaning is the process of maintaining cleanliness and hygiene in a hydroponic system, which is a method of growing plants without soil. Since hydroponic systems rely on nutrient-rich water solutions to deliver essential elements to plants, it is important to keep the system clean to prevent the buildup of algae, mold, and bacteria that can affect plant growth and health.

Here are some tips for cleaning a hydroponic system:

- ➤ Empty the reservoir: Start by emptying the nutrient solution from the reservoir, and dispose of any remaining water and debris.
- ➤ Remove and clean the components: Take out all the system components, such as the pump, tubing, and grow trays, and clean them with a mild soap

solution or hydrogen peroxide. Rinse them thoroughly with clean water and dry them before putting them back in the system.

➤ Scrub the reservoir: Use a scrub brush or sponge to scrub the inside of the reservoir with a mild soap solution or hydrogen peroxide. Rinse the reservoir thoroughly with clean water and let it air dry before adding the fresh nutrient solution.

➤ Monitor pH and nutrient levels: After cleaning the hydroponic system, make sure to monitor the pH and nutrient levels regularly to ensure that the plants are receiving the proper nutrients and that the pH levels are within the optimal range.

6

Best Plants to Grow Hydroponically

There are several plants that can grow very well in a hydroponic system. Here are some of the best plants to grow hydroponically.

Vegetables

Lettuce: Lettuce is one of the most popular hydroponic crops because it is easy to grow, requires minimal maintenance, and has a short growth cycle. Lettuce is a great plant to grow hydroponically because it is easy to grow, fast-growing, and doesn't require a lot of space or nutrients. Here are some of the best lettuce varieties for hydroponic growing:

- ➤ Butterhead lettuce: This type of lettuce has a soft, buttery texture and a mild flavor. It is easy to grow and matures quickly.
- ➤ Romaine lettuce: Romaine lettuce has a crunchy texture and a slightly bitter flavor. It is a good choice for hydroponic growing because it can tolerate a wide range of growing conditions.
- ➤ Looseleaf lettuce: Looseleaf lettuce comes in a variety of colors and has a mild, sweet flavor. It is a fast-growing variety that is easy to harvest.
- ➤ Bibb lettuce: Bibb lettuce has a tender texture and a slightly sweet flavor. It is a slow-growing variety, but it is worth the wait because of its delicate flavor.

When growing lettuce hydroponically, it is important to maintain a pH level of 5.5 to 6.5 and to provide adequate lighting and ventilation. Lettuce also requires a balanced nutrient solution, with the right amount of nitrogen, potassium, and phosphorus. With proper care and attention, lettuce can be a great crop to grow hydroponically.

Spinach: Spinach is another easy-to-grow crop that is perfect for hydroponics. It can be grown all year round and is rich in vitamins and minerals. Spinach is a great plant to grow hydroponically because it grows quickly and can be harvested multiple times. Here are some tips for growing spinach hydroponically:

Choose a variety of spinach that is well-suited for hydroponic growing.

Some popular varieties include:
> New Zealand spinach, Bloomsdale Long Standing spinach, and Corvair spinach.

Start your spinach seeds in a rockwool cube or other hydroponic growing medium. Once the seeds have sprouted, transplant the cubes into your hydroponic system.

Make sure your hydroponic system provides enough light, water, and nutrients for your spinach plants. Spinach prefers a pH range of 6.0 to 7.5 and a temperature range of 50°F to 70°F.

Harvest your spinach when the leaves are large enough to eat, but before they start to yellow or wilt. Spinach can be harvested multiple times, so you can expect to get several harvests from each plant.

Cucumbers: are a great plant to grow hydroponically. Here are some tips to help you get started:

Choose the right variety: There are many varieties of cucumbers available, but some are better suited for hydroponic growing than others. Look for varieties that are known for their compact size, disease resistance, and high yield.

Use a nutrient-rich solution: Cucumbers are heavy feeders and require a nutrient-rich solution to grow properly. You can purchase hydroponic nutrients specifically formulated for cucumbers, or you can mix your own using a blend of macronutrients (nitrogen, phosphorus, and potassium) and micronutrients (calcium, magnesium, iron, etc.).

Provide adequate support: Cucumbers are vine plants and need support to grow vertically. You can use trellises or cages to keep the plants upright and help them produce more fruit.

Control the temperature and humidity: Cucumbers grow best in warm, humid conditions. You may need to adjust the temperature and humidity levels in your hydroponic system to provide the ideal growing conditions.

Prune regularly: Pruning cucumbers can help increase air circulation around the plants and prevent disease. Remove any yellow or damaged leaves, as well as any shoots that are growing from the base of the plant.

Bell peppers: are a great option for growing hydroponically, as they are relatively easy to grow and have a high yield potential. Here are some tips for growing bell peppers hydroponically:

Choose a variety of bell pepper that is well-suited for hydroponic growing. Some good options include California Wonder, Keystone Giant, and Yolo Wonder.

Use a nutrient solution that is formulated for hydroponic growing. Bell peppers need a balanced mix of nitrogen, phosphorus, and potassium, as well as micronutrients like calcium and magnesium.

Choose a hydroponic system that is well-suited for growing bell peppers. Deep water culture, nutrient film technique, and drip irrigation systems are all good options.

Ensure that your hydroponic system has adequate lighting. Bell peppers need at least 12 hours of light per day, and a high-quality LED grow light can help ensure that they get the right amount of light.

Monitor the pH and EC (electrical conductivity) of your nutrient solution regularly. Bell peppers prefer a pH range of 5.5-6.5, and the EC should be kept between 2.0-2.5.

Prune your bell pepper plants regularly to promote bushy growth and increase yield. Pinch off any side shoots that appear on the main stem, and remove any leaves that are blocking light from reaching the lower parts of the plant.

Harvest your bell peppers when they are fully ripe. They should be firm and shiny, with a deep, vibrant color. Harvesting them regularly will encourage the plant to produce more fruit.

Fruits

Tomatoes: Tomatoes are a bit more challenging to grow hydroponically than lettuce and spinach, but they are still a popular choice. They require a little more attention and care, but the rewards are worth it as they produce large yields of juicy, flavorful tomatoes.

Tomatoes are an excellent choice for hydroponic growing, as they can produce high yields and are relatively easy to grow. Here are some of the best types of tomato plants to grow hydroponically:

- ➢ Cherry Tomatoes - Cherry tomatoes are compact, produce fruit quickly, and are perfect for hydroponic growing.
- ➢ Beefsteak Tomatoes - Beefsteak tomatoes are large, juicy, and flavorful. They require a bit more

space, but can still be grown successfully in a hydroponic system.

➢ Roma Tomatoes - Roma tomatoes are smaller and have a firmer texture, making them ideal for sauces and canning. They are also great for hydroponic growing.

➢ Heirloom Tomatoes - Heirloom tomatoes come in a wide range of colors and flavors, and can be grown successfully in hydroponic systems.

When growing tomatoes hydroponically, it's important to provide adequate support for the plants as they grow, as well as proper lighting, temperature, and nutrient levels. With the right care and attention, you can grow healthy and delicious tomatoes all year round.

Strawberries can be grown hydroponically and can thrive in this type of environment. Here are some of the best varieties to grow hydroponically:

➢ Albion: This is a popular variety for hydroponic cultivation because it produces large, firm fruit with excellent flavor. It's also disease-resistant and has a long shelf life.

➢ Chandler: This variety is known for its high yield and large, sweet fruit. It's also disease-resistant and has a long harvest season.

➢ Seascape: This variety produces large, juicy fruit with a sweet flavor. It's also disease-resistant and has a high yield.

> ➤ Evie 2: This variety produces large, firm fruit with a sweet flavor. It's also disease-resistant and has a long harvest season.

When growing strawberries hydroponically, it's important to provide them with the proper nutrients and pH levels. The ideal pH range for strawberries is between 5.5 and 6.5, and they require a balanced nutrient solution that includes nitrogen, phosphorus, potassium, and micronutrients. Providing the plants with adequate light and a suitable growing environment is also important for their growth and productivity.

Blueberries can be grown hydroponically, but they can be challenging to cultivate because they have specific requirements for pH, nutrient levels, and temperature. Here are some tips on how to successfully grow blueberries hydroponically:

Choose the right variety: Not all blueberry varieties are suitable for hydroponic growing. Choose a variety that is known to perform well in containers and has a compact growth habit.

Optimize pH levels: Blueberries prefer acidic soil, so it's important to maintain a pH of between 4.5 and 5.5 in your hydroponic system. Use pH testing kits to monitor and adjust the pH levels regularly.

Provide adequate nutrients: Blueberries require a balanced nutrient solution with a specific ratio of nitrogen, phosphorus, and potassium. Use a hydroponic nutrient solution formulated specifically for blueberries, and adjust the nutrient levels as necessary.

Control temperature: Blueberries grow best in cool temperatures, ideally between 60 and 70 degrees Fahrenheit. Make sure to provide adequate ventilation and use a cooling system to maintain a consistent temperature. Provide adequate lighting: Blueberries require at least 12 hours of full-spectrum light per day. Use grow lights to supplement natural light and ensure that the plants receive adequate light.

Melons can be challenging to grow hydroponically, but it is possible with the right setup and technique. Here are some tips for growing melons hydroponically:

Choose the right variety: Not all melon varieties are suitable for hydroponic growing. Look for compact or bush varieties that are more manageable in size and easier to train up a trellis. Some good options include Cantaloupe, Honeydew, and Watermelon.

Start with healthy seedlings: Start with healthy seedlings that are disease-free and have a strong root system. Melons can be sensitive to transplant shock, so handle them carefully when transplanting.

Provide adequate support: Melons are heavy, and their vines can break under the weight of the fruit. Provide adequate support by trellising them and using clips to hold the vines in place.

Optimize growing conditions: Melons thrive in warm temperatures and require plenty of light to grow. Ensure that your hydroponic system provides sufficient lighting, temperature, and humidity levels to promote healthy growth.

Provide proper nutrients: Melons are heavy feeders and require a nutrient-rich solution to grow. Use a balanced hydroponic nutrient solution that provides essential macro and micronutrients.

Pollination: Melons require pollination to produce fruit. In hydroponic systems, you can hand-pollinate the flowers with a small brush or by shaking the plant gently.

Herbs

Basil is a wonderful herb to grow in hydroponics. It is simple to cultivate, yields a large amount, and may be used in a variety of cuisines.

- Fast-growing: Basil grows quickly, which makes it an ideal herb to grow hydroponically. You can enjoy fresh basil in just a few weeks.
- Low-maintenance: Basil is easy to care for and does not require a lot of attention. It does not need soil and can grow well in a hydroponic system.
- High yield: Basil can produce a high yield of leaves, which makes it a great herb to grow hydroponically.

Chives are a great herb to grow hydroponically because they are easy to grow and require minimal maintenance. Here are some tips on how to successfully grow chives hydroponically:

Choose a nutrient-rich hydroponic solution: Chives require a balanced blend of nutrients to grow properly. You can find pre-mixed nutrient solutions at a hydroponics store, or you can mix your own using a recipe that includes all the necessary nutrients.

Use a suitable growing medium: Chives grow best in a lightweight, well-draining growing medium. Perlite, vermiculite, and coconut coir are all good choices for hydroponic chive growing.

Provide adequate lighting: Chives require bright, direct light to grow properly. If you don't have access to natural sunlight, consider using artificial grow lights to provide the necessary light for your plants.

Maintain proper pH levels: Chives grow best in a pH range of 6.0 to 7.0. Regularly check the pH levels of your nutrient solution and adjust as necessary to ensure optimal growth.

Monitor water levels: Chives prefer to be kept slightly moist, but not waterlogged. Be sure to monitor the water levels in your hydroponic system and adjust as necessary to prevent overwatering.

Cilantro is a popular herb to grow hydroponically, as it is easy to grow and provides fresh, flavorful leaves for use in a variety of dishes. Here are some tips on how to grow cilantro hydroponically:

Start with high-quality cilantro seeds. You can purchase these online or at a local gardening store.

Choose a hydroponic system that is suitable for growing herbs. There are many different types of hydroponic systems available, such as deep water culture, nutrient film technique, and drip irrigation.

Use a high-quality hydroponic nutrient solution that is specifically designed for herbs. This will provide your cilantro with the essential nutrients it needs to grow.
Maintain the proper pH level in your hydroponic system. Cilantro prefers a pH between 6.0 and 7.0.
Provide your cilantro with the right amount of light. Cilantro requires at least six hours of direct sunlight or 12 hours of artificial light per day.
Monitor the temperature and humidity levels in your hydroponic system. Cilantro prefers a temperature range of 60 to 75 degrees Fahrenheit and a humidity level of 50 to 70 percent.
Harvest your cilantro regularly to encourage new growth. Cut the stems just above the bottom set of leaves, leaving some of the stem intact to encourage new growth.

Mint is an excellent herb to grow hydroponically because it is easy to cultivate, fast-growing, and very hardy. Here are some tips on growing mint hydroponically:
Choose a variety of mint that is suitable for hydroponic growing, such as peppermint, spearmint, or chocolate mint.
Start with healthy, disease-free cuttings or seedlings. You can purchase these from a local nursery or garden center, or start them from seed yourself.
Use a nutrient-rich hydroponic solution to feed your mint plants. The ideal pH range for mint is between 6.0 and 7.0, and the EC should be between 1.6 and 2.2.

Mint plants prefer cooler temperatures, so keep the temperature of your hydroponic system between 60 and 75 degrees Fahrenheit.

Provide adequate lighting for your mint plants. They need at least 12 to 16 hours of light each day, and LED grow lights are an excellent option for indoor hydroponic systems.

Monitor your mint plants for pests and diseases. Aphids, spider mites, and whiteflies are common pests that can infest mint plants, while fungal diseases like powdery mildew and downy mildew can also be a problem.

Oregano is a great herb to grow hydroponically as it is easy to maintain, grows quickly, and has many culinary uses. Here are some tips for growing oregano hydroponically:

Start with healthy plants: Purchase healthy oregano seedlings or cuttings from a reputable nursery or garden center.

Choose a suitable hydroponic system: Oregano can be grown in most hydroponic systems, including deep water culture, nutrient film technique, and drip irrigation. Choose a system that suits your growing space and budget.

Provide adequate lighting: Oregano requires at least 12-14 hours of light per day to grow and thrive. Supplemental lighting may be necessary if natural light is insufficient.

Maintain optimal temperature and humidity: Oregano grows best in temperatures between 65-75°F (18-24°C) and relative humidity of 50-60%.

Use a suitable growing medium: Oregano can be grown in a variety of growing media, including coconut coir, rockwool, perlite, or vermiculite.

Provide adequate nutrients: Use a high-quality hydroponic nutrient solution that provides all the essential nutrients for plant growth, including nitrogen, phosphorus, and potassium.

Monitor pH and EC levels: Oregano prefers a pH range between 6.0-7.0 and an EC range between 1.0-2.0 mS/cm.

Prune regularly: Regular pruning will encourage bushy growth and prevent the plant from becoming too leggy.

Parsley is an excellent herb to grow hydroponically as it thrives in a soilless environment and requires minimal maintenance. Here are some tips for growing parsley hydroponically:

Choose the right variety: Curly parsley is the most common variety, but Italian flat-leaf parsley is also a good choice for hydroponic growing.

Use a deep-water culture (DWC) system: This type of hydroponic system is ideal for growing parsley as it allows the roots to be submerged in nutrient-rich water, promoting healthy growth.

Provide adequate lighting: Parsley requires at least 6-8 hours of sunlight per day, so make sure your hydroponic setup has enough artificial lighting to provide this amount of light.

Maintain the proper nutrient balance: Parsley needs a balanced blend of macronutrients (nitrogen, phosphorus, and potassium) and micronutrients (calcium, magnesium, iron, and others) to grow well. Make sure you use a high-quality hydroponic nutrient solution and monitor the pH levels of the water regularly.

Keep the water temperature consistent: Parsley grows best in water that is between 60-75°F (15-24°C), so make sure the water in your hydroponic setup stays within this range.